D1758179

CHRISTMAS TREAT RECIPE BOOK

Quick and Easy Timeless Delicious Mouthwatering Sweet Fun Christmas Dessert Cookbooks for the Holidays- Fudges, Toffees, Candies, Cookies, Cakes and Many mores

CHAPTER 01: FUDGE:

01. CANDY CANE FUDGE

Prep:20 mins

Additional:2 hrs Total: Two hours 20 mins

Servings: 64 Yield:2 1/4 pounds

Ingredients:

- 2 (10 ounces) packages of vanilla baking chips
- 1 (14 ounces) can sweeten condensed milk
- ½ tsp peppermint extract
- 1 ½ cups of crushed candy canes
- One dash of red or green food coloring

Directions:

Step 1

- Grease an 8-inch square baking pan and line it with aluminum foil.

Step 2

- Bring the sweetened condensed milk and vanilla chips to a boil in a saucepan. Take off the heat and stir in the salt. Take the pan from the heat and continue to whisk until the mixture is completely melted. Mix in the peppermint extract, food coloring, and candy canes when the chips are all melted.

Step 3

- Evenly distribute the mixture to the bottom of the pan. Cut into squares after chilling for two hours.

Nutrition Facts

Per Serving: 89 calories; protein 1.1g; carbohydrates 14.1g; fat 2.9g; cholesterol 2.1mg; sodium 27.4mg.

02. EASY PEANUT BUTTER FUDGE

yield: ABOUT 25 PIECES cook time: 5 MINUTES prep time: 5 MINUTES additional time: 1 HOUR total time: 1 HOUR 10 MINUTES

INGREDIENTS

- 2 cups of granulated Sugar
- ½ cup of milk
- 1 tsp vanilla
- ¾ cup of peanut butter

INSTRUCTIONS

- An 8x8 baking dish should be lightly sprayed with nonstick-stick cooking spray before use.
- In a medium Pan, Mix the milk and Sugar. Bring to a boil over medium-low heat. After 2   ½ minutes, continue to boil, constantly stirring to avoid sticking.
- To finish it off, remove it from heat and whisk in the butter, vanilla, and peanut butter until smooth.
- Let cool entirely in the prepared pan before serving.

Nutrition Information:

Yield: 25 Serving Size: 1

Amount Per Serving: Calories: 110Total Fat: 4g Saturated Fat: 1g Trans Fat: 0g Unsaturated Fat: 3g Cholesterol: 0mg Sodium: 40 mg Carbohydrates: 18gFPound er: 0gSugar: 16gProtein: 2g

03. PEPPERMINT CRUNCH FUDGE

Prep Time:15 minutes

Total Time:15 minutes

Servings: 64 pieces

Ingredients

- Chocolate Layer:

- 14 Ounces can, sweetened condensed milk
- Three c. semisweet chocolate chips
- 1 tsp. peppermint extract

Peppermint Layer:

- 14 Ounces can, sweetened condensed milk
- Three cups white chocolate chips
- 1 tsp. peppermint extract
- red food coloring a few drops

Topping:

- 1/2 c. mini chocolate chips
- 1/2 c. peppermint crunch like Andes Mints Peppermint Crunch Baking Bits

Instructions

- Draw a 9-by-9-inch grid in pencil "Spray nonstick-stick cooking spray lightly on the baking pan and line with aluminum foil. Dispose of.
- Add the chocolate chips and one can of sweetened condensed milk to a microwave-safe bowl. Stir the mixture for a minute on high heat. Stir until the chocolate chunks are completely melted and the mixture is smooth. Add the peppermint oil and mix well. As the mixture cools, it will thicken. Prepare a thin layer of the mixture on the bottom of the prepared baking dish.
- White chocolate chips and the second can of sweetened condensed milk go into the creation of the double pink layer—heat on high for one minute in the microwave. Stir. They are constantly stirring, heat for 30 seconds at a time until the chocolate chunks are melted. Keep an eye on your body's internal temperature. Stir in a few drops of red food coloring and a few drops of peppermint extract until the mixture is bright pink. On top of the

chocolate, use a pastry brush to create a decorative border.

- Sprinkle tiny chocolate chips and peppermint crunch on top for added flavor. Before chopping, let the food sit in the refrigerator for at least two hours. Lift the fudge out of the pan using the foil sides to make cutting it more accessible. Make a 14-inch cut "the shape of a square.

Nutrition Facts:

Calories: 183kcal | Carbohydrates: 21g | Protein: 2g | Fat: 9g | Saturated Fat: 6g | Cholesterol: 7mg | Sodium: 29mg | Potassium: 140mg | Sugar: 19g |

04. OLD FASHIONED HARD FUDGE

ready in:30-60 minutes serves/makes:2 lbs

ingredients:

- 3 cups of Sugar
- 2/3 cup of cocoa powder
- 1/8 tsp salt
- 1 1/2 cup of milk
- 1/4 cup of butter
- 1 tsp vanilla extract

directions:

- Use aluminum foil to line an 8- or 9-inch square baking tray—butter the aluminum foil generously.
- In a big, heavy saucepan, combine the sugar, cocoa powder, and salt over medium heat. Stir the ingredients together thoroughly. Rather than a whisk, use a wooden spoon to stir in the milk. Maintain a rolling boil over high heat while going regularly. Allow it to simmer, uncovered until a candy thermometer reads 234 degrees Fahrenheit (softball stage, drop a little amount in very cold water to

test it - it should form a softball that flattens when removed from the water).

- Turn off the warm and take the pan. Do not stir the saucepan after adding the butter and vanilla. To reach a temperature of 110-120 degrees Fahrenheit, simply let the mixture settle.
- When the fudge has cooled, use a wooden spoon to whip it until it has thickened and lost part of its shine. Spread the fudge in the prepared pan as quickly as possible. Allow to cool completely before cutting into squares (do not attempt to speed up the cooling process, or it may not be set up properly). Refrigerate the fudge after it has been wrapped loosely in foil.

cook's notes:

- Vanilla can be replaced with other flavor extracts (peppermint, caramel, strawberry, coffee, etc.). Dried fruit and nuts can be added to the pudding as it sets. Fudge will not harden correctly if you use margarine because of its high water content.

Nutrition:

Ninety-seven calories, 2 grams fat, 20 grams carbohydrates, 1 gram protein per ounce.

5. WHITE CHOCOLATE PEPPERMINT FUDGE

PREP TIME:1 min
COOK TIME:1 min TOTAL SERVINGS:40

INGREDIENTS:

- 3 cups of white chocolate chips
- One 14-Ounces can sweeten condensed milk
- 1 tsp peppermint extract

- ¼ tsp sea salt
- crushed peppermint candies for topping

INSTRUCTIONS:

- White chocolate chips and condensed milk should be mixed in a big microwavable bowl before reheating in 15-second intervals—no more than a minute at the most.
- Add sea salt and peppermint extract.
- Pour melted white chocolate into a 9x9 or 8x8 baking pan, smooth with a spatula, and top with peppermint candies.
- Let the meat cool completely before chopping it into 1-inch chunks

NUTRITION

Calories: 73kcal

06. HOT CHOCOLATE FUDGE

Yield:24 Pieces
Prep Time:10 minutes
Total Time:4 hours 10 minutes

Ingredients:

- 2 and 1/2 cups of semisweet chocolate chips
- One packet of hot chocolate mix
- 14 ounces sweetened condensed milk
- 1 tsp vanilla extract
- 1 cup of cereal marshmallows

Directions:

- Spray an 8x8 pot with vegetable oil spray and line with foil.
- Then add the chocolate chunks and sweetened condensed milk to the simmering water.
- Take from heat and stir in the chocolate until smooth.

- Add vanilla extract when the chocolate mixture is completely smooth.
- Make sure to spread the fudge evenly in the baking pan.
- Add a layer of cereal marshmallows and carefully press them in.
- Slicing should take place at least four hours after being refrigerated.

Nutrition:

Calories: 173kcal | Carbohydrates: 21g | Protein: 2g | Fat: 9g | Saturated Fat: 5g | Cholesterol: 7mg | Sodium: 25mg | Potassium: 168mg | FPound er: 2g | Sugar: 17g | Vitamin A: 54IU | Vitamin C: 1mg | Calcium: 59mg | Iron: 1mg

CHAPTER 02:COOKIES

07. CHEWY BUTTERFINGER COOKIES

Prep Time: 15 minutes
Cook Time:10 minutes
Total Time: 45 minutes Yield: 30 cookies

Ingredients:

- One and 3/4 cups of all-purpose flour (spoon & leveled)
- 3/4 tsp baking soda
- 1/4 tsp salt
- 3/4 cup of granulated Sugar
- 1/2 cup of salted butter, softened to room temperature
- One large egg, at room temperature
- Eight fun-sized Butterfinger candy bars, chopped

Instructions:

- Warm up the oven to 350°F (177°C).
- In a small basin, whisk together the flour, baking soda, and salt; place aside. Batter the Sugar and butter together

with an electric mixer until they are light and fluffy. Beat in the egg one at a time until it's incorporated.

- Slowly add flour mixture into the batter. By hand, add the Butterfinger bits. You can expect the dough to be relatively dense. Drop by the tablespoonful onto an uncoated baking sheet.
- Place in the microwave and Roast for 10-12 minutes, until the top is just starting to turn golden. Cool fully on a wire rack.

Notes:

- PREPARE AHEAD OF TIME & FREEZE FOR UP TO A WEEK. IN AN AIRTIGHT CONTAINER, COOKIES CAN BE KEPT AT ROOM TEMPERATURE FOR UP TO A WEEK. BAKED COOKIES CAN BE KEPT IN THE Refrigerator FOR UP TO THREE MONTHS. UNBAKED COOKIE DOUGH BALLS CAN BE KEPT IN THE FREEZER FOR UP TO THREE MONTHS.NO NO NEED TO THAW THE FROZEN frOuncesen cookie dough balls; bake them for an additional minute.

08. CHRISTMAS GOOEY BUTTER COOKIES

PREP TIME: One HOUR 15 MINUTES
COOK TIME:10 MINUTES
TOTAL TIME: One HOUR 25 MINUTES SERVINGS:42 SMALL COOKIES

Ingredients:

- 1/2 c. unsalted butter room temperature
- 1 8 Ounces. pkg. cream cheese, room temperature
- One egg
- 1/2 tsp. Almond extract opt.
- 1/2 tsp. Orange extract opt.

- One pkg. white cake mix
- 1/2 c. sprinkles divided
- 1/2 c. powdered Sugar

Instructions

- Cream the butter and cream cheese until frothy. Add the egg, almond extract, and orange extract, and mix until well incorporated. Mix the white cake mix into the batter until it's evenly distributed. Sprinkle in 14 cups of the sprinkles, if desired. Freeze for one hour or up to 24 hours, wrapped in plastic. The less sticky the dough becomes, the longer it is allowed to chill.
- The oven should be Warn up to 350 degrees Fahrenheit. One bowl should contain powdered Sugar, and the other should have the remaining 14 cups of sprinkles. Cookie dough can be rolled into balls using the 1-inch cookie scoop. Add a few more sprinkles and roll the dough ball in powdered sugar to cover it completely. Spray a cookie sheet with nonstick-stick cooking spray. Repeat—Time the oven to 10 minutes. Take cookies from baking pan to wire rack after two minutes of cooling time on cookie sheet. About 42 tiny cookies are produced.

Nutritions:

Calories91kcal (5%) Carbohydrates15g (5%) Protein1g (2%) Fat3g (5%)

09. CARAMEL CHOCOLATE CHIP COOKIES

PREP TIME: 10 minutes
COOK TIME: 10 minutes
TOTAL TIME: 20 minutes SERVINGS: 40 COOKIES

Ingredients:

- 1 cup of (2 sticks) unsalted butter, softened
- 1 cup of granulated white Sugar

- 1 cup of packed Brown Sugar
- Two large eggs
- 2 tsp vanilla extract
- 1 tsp baking soda
- 1 tsp salt
- 3 cups of all-purpose flour
- 3/4 cup of semisweet chocolate chips
- 3/4 cup of caramel chips

Instructions:

- Cook at 375 degrees Fahrenheit in a preheated oven for about 30 minutes. To begin, prepare the baking sheets by lining them with parchment paper.
- In a Big Pot, Mix the butter, sugar, eggs, and vanilla essence. One min with an electric mixer until smooth and creamy.
- The baking soda, salt, and flour should be mixed in a medium-sized bowl. Add the dry elements to the butter/sugar mixture gradually, mixing at low speed. It's time to scrape the bowl and continue beating on medium-high speed for another 30 seconds until the mixture is smooth.
- When the dough has been rolled out, add the chocolate and caramel chips and stir to blend. Dollop dough onto prepared baking sheets, spreading them 2-3 inches apart. Take the cookies from the oven and cool them slightly before placing them on a wire rack to cool completely. Enjoy!

Nutrition

Calories: 157kcal | Carbohydrates: 21g | Protein: 1g | Fat: 7g | Saturated Fat: 4g | Cholesterol: 20mg | Sodium: 131mg | Potassium: 60mg | Sugar: 12g |

10. EGGNOG COOKIES

Prep Time8 minutes Cook Time11 minutes Total Time19 minutes Servings18 cookies

Ingredients:

- Two ¼ cups of all-purpose flour (270g)
- 1 1/2 tsp baking powder
- 1/2 tsp salt
- 1/2 tsp ground nutmeg
- 1/2 tsp ground cinnamon
- 3/4 cup of unsalted butter, at room temperature (170g)
- 1 cup of granulated sugar (200g)
- Two egg yolks
- 2 tsp vanilla extract
- 1/2 cup of eggnog

For the optional glaze:

- 1 cup of powdered Sugar
- 3 tbsp eggnog
- ¼ tsp cinnamon
- ¼ tsp nutmeg
- 1 tsp vanilla extract

Instructions

- Gather the ingredients for the batter in a medium-sized bowl and mix thoroughly.
- You may use a stand mixer with a paddle attachment or an electric hand mixer to whip the Butter and Sugar together. Batter on high speed with a mixer until the mixture is light and fluffy.
- Gather your ingredients and begin by pouring the eggnog and vanilla into the basin, followed by the egg yolks one at a time. Scrape the bowl and stir one more.

- At a low speed, add the flour until barely combined. Using a spatula, gently fold in any remaining butter or flour.
- Each piece should be around two tablespoons in size and placed on a parchment or silicone-lined baking sheet with about four inches of space in between each. For a more polished look, you can roll each ball with your palms. When the borders are firmly set, and the center appears to be dry, bake at 350F for 11-12 minutes in the center rack.
- Gather your ingredients for the glaze while your cookies are in the oven. In a medium bowl, combine 1 cup powdered sugar, cinnamon, and nutmeg. Drizzle in 3 tablespoons eggnog and one teaspoon vanilla. You may need to add additional eggnog as needed to obtain the desired dripping consistency by slowly whisking the eggnog into the mixture.
- Once the cookies have cooled, drizzle the frosting over them.

Notes:

- There is no need to chill the dough, but you can do so ahead of time if you choose.
- For optimal results, use a scale to measure your flour. Luff the flour and sprinkle it into your measuring cup before leveling if you do not have one.
- Make sure your cookies are all the same size so that they cook evenly. The cookies will spread if you use more than two tablespoons of cookie batter.
- Allow approximately 10 minutes for the cookies to cool on the baking sheet before transferring them to a cooling rack.
- To enhance the flavor of your eggnog, you can use a half-tsp of rum extract or Add a few drops of rum liquor.

- As the cookies are baking, you can make the glaze.
- Keep cookies in an airtight container.

Nutrition
Calories: 212kcal | Carbohydrates: 31g | Protein: 2g | Fat: 9g | Saturated Fat: 5g | Cholesterol: 48mg | Sodium: 139mg | Potassium: 79mg | FPound er: 1g | Sugar: 19g | Vitamin A: 285IU | Vitamin C: 1mg | Calcium: 38mg | Iron: 1mg

11. GRINCH CRINKLE COOKIES
PREP TIME:10 MINUTES
COOK TIME: Eight MINUTES TOTAL TIME:20 MINUTES
SERVINGS: 18 TO 24 COOKIES

Equipment:
- Baking sheets
- NonstickNon-stick silicone mat
- Parchment paper (precut)
- Mixing bowls
- Whisk
- KitchenAid Stand Mixer
- Food coloring gel paste
- Cookie scoops

Wire cooling racks

INGREDIENTS:
- 2 ½ cups of all-purpose flour
- 1 ½ cups of Granulated Sugar
- 1 Tbsp + 1 tsp baking powder
- 1 tsp kosher salt
- ¼ cup of unsalted butter softened
- Two large eggs, room temperature
- ⅓ cup of unsalted butter, melted (or oil)
- 1 Tbsp pure vanilla extract
- 1 tsp mint extract, or less, as need

- Green gel food coloring paste
- Heart-shaped sprinkles, aff link

Directions:

- Warm-up oven to 375°F and line two baking sheets with parchment paper or silicone mats. Get rid of it.
- Mix flour, sugar, baking powder, and salt.
- With a pastry blender, mix
- in the softened butter until a fine crumb form.
- Mix flour, eggs, melted butter, vanilla extract, and mint extract in a stand mixer fitted with a paddle attachment until well blended.
- Combine in a few drops of gel paste until the dough comes together. Keep in mind that the color will fade a little while baking, so adds additional food coloring if necessary.
- No more than nine dough balls should be placed on each prepared baking sheet when using a medium cookie scoop (they need room to spread while baking).
- Shape each dough ball into a smooth ball by rolling it in your palms and pressing down gently on the top. Eight minutes in the oven is a good starting point; the cookies will continue to wrinkle as they cool.
- As soon as the cookies are taken out of the oven, sprinkle a heart sprinkle on top of each one. Remove from oven and allow excellent for a few minutes before transferring to wire racks to finish cooling. Enjoy!

NOTES:

- You can use a box of white cake mix in place of the first four ingredients if you like. There is a difference in the size of the eggs you utilize. You may lose some moisture if they are smaller in size. You can add a bit of additional melted butter or oil if your mixture is too dry.

NUTRITION

s Facts:

Carbohydrates: 30g Protein: 2g Calories: 191kcal Fat: 7g
Saturated Fat: 4g FPound er: 1g Sugar: 17g

12. HOT CHOCOLATE COOKIES

Prep Time: 15 minutesCook Time: 9 minutesTotal Time: 24
minutes Servings: 20

Ingredients:

- ½ cup softened unsalted butter
- ⅔ cup of packed light brown sugar, make sure it's fresh and soft
- ⅓ cup of granulated Sugar
- One large egg
- 1 tsp pure vanilla extract
- ⅓ cup of unsweetened cocoa
- 1 cup of plus 2 tbsp all-purpose flour*
- ½ tsp baking soda
- ¼ tsp salt
- 1 tsp cornstarch
- 1 cup of chocolate chips, divided
- Ten full-size marshmallows, cut in half across the middle
- 2 tbsp finely chopped chocolate (for topping), optional

Instructions:

- Preheat oven to 350°F.
- Cover two baking sheets with parchment. Whip the butter and sugars into a light and fluffy texture using a hand or stand mixer fitted with a paddle attachment. Scrape down the bowl as you add the egg and vanilla.
- When you're done with the cocoa powder and the other dry ingredients, you'll need to add the cornstarch. In a

low-speed mixer, gradually add the flour mixture to the butter mixture until it is completely incorporated. To decorate the dough balls, set aside 14 cups of the chocolate chips; use the remaining 34 cups of chocolate chips in the batter.

- Using a cookie scoop, divide the dough into 1-½ tbsp sections and place on the cookie sheets. Make sure the dough balls are piled up a good deal (not flattened). Every dough ball should have some of the remaining chocolate chips sprinkled on top of it.
- There should still be an intact mound of cookie dough in the center of the cookie after baking for 7-8 minutes**. As soon as the cookies are out of the oven, gently press one half of a marshmallow into the top of each one. This will help to flatten the cookies just a little bit more. Bake for an additional 1-2 minutes. Even if the edges look a little undercooked, that's fine. When you take them out of the oven, they should appear undercooked, not fully baked. Wire racks can be used to cool the baking sheets fully (the cookies will firm up as they cool). If preferred, top each biscuit with a little amount of chopped chocolate while they're still warm. Once the baking pans have cooled, use the remaining dough to make another batch of cookies.

Notes:

*To properly measure flour: Fluff the flour with your measuring cup, scoop a generous piece, then use a knife to level it to achieve the proper amount of flour.

- Your dough balls may need to be cooked longer or shorter, depending on their size. Take care not to overcook your food.
- Between batches, you may wish to put the dough in the fridge to keep it cool.

Serving:

- While the chocolate chips and marshmallows are soft and gooey, I prefer to serve these cookies somewhat warm. Baked goods should be served within two days of being baked.

Storage:

- Cookies can be kept covered for two days at room temperature. Unbaked cookie dough can be frozen for up to two months.

Nutrition Facts:

Protein: 2g Fat: 7g Calories: 168kcal Carbohydrates: 25g Saturated Fat: 4g Cholesterol: 22mg Sodium: 72mg Potassium: 41mg FPound er: 1g

13. MINT OREO PUDDING COOKIES

Ingredients

- 1 cup of butter softened
- 1/2 cup of brown Sugar
- 1/2 cup of Sugar
- 1 4.2 Ounces pkg Oreo Cookies & Cream pudding mix
- Two eggs
- 1 tsp vanilla extract
- 1 tsp mint extract
- 2 1/4 cups of flour
- One tsp baking soda
- Three drops blue food coloring 10-12 drops green food coloring
- 15 Mint Oreo cookies or regular Oreos - they work great too! coarsely crushed (you want big chunks!)

Instructions:

- THE BUTTER AND SUGARS SHOULD BE CREAMED TOGETHER WITH A HAND MIXER.MIX IN THE PUDDING MIX UNTIL IT'S COMPLETELY INCORPORATED.

- Then, whisk in the egg whites, vanilla essence, and mint extract.

- Continue mixing after adding the flour and baking soda.

- DOUGHS SHOULD BE COLORED TO THE APPROPRIATE SHADE BY MIXING IN FOOD COLORING.

- MIX IN THE CHUNKS OF THE OREO COOKIE.

- Drop cookies onto a greased cookie sheet in rounded tablespoonfuls (I use a cookie scoop). You'll need to bake for ten minutes at 350 degrees Fahrenheit. Enjoy!

14. PEPPERMINT KISS COOKIES

PREP TIME: 20 mins
COOK TIME: 10 mins
TOTAL TIME: 30 mins

INGREDIENTS:

- 2 cups of all-purpose flour
- 2 tsp baking powder
- 1/2 tsp salt
- 1/2 cup of unsalted butter - softened
- 3/4 cup of sugar, plus 1/2 cup of for garnish
- Two eggs
- 1 tsp vanilla extract
- 1 tbsp plus 1 tsp coarse green sugar*
- 1 tbsp plus 1 tsp coarse red Sugar*
- 36 Peppermint Kisses - unwrapped

INSTRUCTIONS:

- Before you start cooking, warm up your oven to 350°F.
- A pot Mix well the flour, baking powder, and salt

. Delete.

- Using a mixer, Batter the butter and sugar together until light and fluffy. This should be quick. Then add the eggs one by one. Add vanilla essence.
- Stir in the dry ingredients until barely combined. Divide the dough into two bowls. Make a single bowl of dough by adding one tbsp of green Sugar and mixing it with a spoon. One tablespoon of red Sugar can be added at this point to the second bowl of dough and mixed in.
- In two separate shallow bowls, divide the remaining 1/2 cup of sugar evenly. One teaspoon of green Sugar and one teaspoon of red Sugar should be added to the two bowls.
- Make 1-inch dough balls with a spoon or a cookie scoop. Make a ball out of the dough by rolling it in the palm of your hand. After that, use the contrasting colored Sugar to coat the dough ball. (Green dough is colored green, and the red dough is colored red.) Sugar-coated dough balls should be placed on a cookie sheet. Rep with the remaining dough.
- Gently flatten each dough ball with your finger before baking—Bake for 8 to 10 minutes.
- Cool the cookies on a wire rack after they have been removed from the oven. Allow the cookies to cool for two to three minutes before adding a peppermint kiss to each one. To prevent the cookies from melting, wait until they are completely cold before handling or moving them. Refrigerate the cookies in an airtight container.
- The more colored Sugar you use, the better. Divide the dough into equal portions.

NUTRITION FACTS

Calories: 91kcal • Carbohydrates: 12g • Protein: 1g • Fat: 4g •
Saturated Fat: 2g • Cholesterol: 17mg • Sodium: 64mg •
Potassium: 11mg • FPound er: 1g • Sugar: 7g

15. RED VELVET COOKIES

Prep Time: 10 minutes
Cook Time: 15 minutes Chill Time 30 minutes Total Time 55
minutes Servings12 cookies

Equipment:

- Baking Sheet

Ingredients

- 1 cup of unsalted butter 226g
- 1 cup of granulated sugar 200g
- One egg
- 2 tsp vanilla extract 10mL
- 2 cups of all-purpose flour 240g
- ¼ cup of cocoa powder 25g
- ½ tsp baking soda
- ½ tsp baking powder
- ¼ tsp kosher salt
- 1 Tbsp hot brewed coffee 15mL
- 1 tbsp liquid red food coloring 15mL
- 3/4 cup of chopped semisweet chocolate chips 130g
- 12 ounces cream cheese softened, 340g
- 1 cup of powdered sugar sifted, 100g
- 2 Tbsp milk or heavy cream 30mL
- 1 cup of white chocolate chips 150g

Instructions:

- Pour the flour, cocoa, and salt into a bowl and whisk them together. Then, add the baking soda and baking powder, and mix them.

- Using a hand mixer, whip the butter and sugar together until light and fluffy, about 2 minutes. Egg and vanilla should be included in the mix.
- Mix flour and butter on low speed until barely mixed.
- The coffee and red food coloring should be mixed thoroughly. (don't go over the top)
- Add 1 cup of chopped chocolate to the mixture.
- Put the dough in the fridge for 30 minutes.
- Using a 1 tbsp scoop, gently roll the dough into balls and place them on a baking sheet. Roll the dough into 2-inch-wide balls and place on a rimmed baking pan.
- Roast at 350° for 10 to 12 minutes, or until the edges are crisp.
- The cookies should be cooled before being transferred to a wire rack.
- Blend the powdered sugar and cream cheese with a stand or hand mixer until smooth. If desired, add milk or heavy cream and mix well.
- Fill half of the cookies with about 1 tbsp of filling. Bottom-sides-up, place the rest of the cookies on top.
- For the smoothness of the white chocolate:
- Microwave the white chocolate in 30-second intervals in a small bowl (about three times).
- A Ziploc bag with melted white chocolate is all that is needed for this recipe. Snip the bag's corner and use it to sprinkle cookies, whichever you like. Cookies should be frozen for around 15 minutes to harden the chocolate.

Notes:

- - You can make these cookies more quickly and easily if you use a spring-loaded 1-tbsp scoop. To ensure that your cookie dough balls are all the same size, you can use a scoop to make them. - Roll the sandwich cookies into balls with your hands before baking to provide a lovely round form. After drizzling the top of the cookies with chocolate, put them in the freezer for a few minutes to harden. Spread the cream cheese filling over the bottoms of the cookies, then top with the drizzly-dipped tops. - If you prefer your cookies to be a little sweeter, you can add more powdered sugar to the cream cheese filling.

Nutrition

Serving: 1cookie | Calories: 304kcal | Carbohydrates: 34g | Protein: 6g | Fat: 31g | Saturated Fat: 11g | Cholesterol: 69mg | Sodium: 107mg | Potassium: 108mg | FPound er: 1g | Sugar: 36g | Vitamin A: 478IU

CHAPTER 3:TREAT AND CANDIES:

16. CANDIED PECANS

Prep Time: 5 minutes

Cook Time: 15 minutes

Total Time: 20 minutes Yield Yield: 3 cups of

Ingredients:

- 2 tbsp salted butter
- 3 cups of pecan halves
- 1/2 cup of light brown Sugar
- 1/2 tsp cinnamon
- 1 tsp kosher salt or sea salt
- 1/4 cup of water
- 1 tsp vanilla

Instructions

- Preheat oven to 350°F. To begin, prepare a baking sheet by lining it with parchment paper.

- Melt the butter in a big skillet. Continue stirring for 3 minutes until the pecans are gently toasted.
- For an additional 2 minutes, add the brown sugar and whisk to dissolve the Sugar.
- Salt and pepper should be dissolved in water, then cinnamon and water should be mixed in.
- Take care not to overcook; the water should evaporate in a matter of minutes.
- Mix the vanilla into the batter and coat it thoroughly.
- To bake, remove from the oven and spread evenly on the baking sheet.
- Bake for 5-7 minutes, or until fragrant and faintly crisped.
- Cool thoroughly on a baking sheet after taking from the oven.

Notes:

• Keep at room temperature for up to 7 days in an airtight container.

Nutrition Information:

Serving Size: 1/4 cup of Calories: 212 Sugar: 6.9 g Sodium: 17.1 mg Fat: 19.7 g Carbohydrates: 9.5 g Protein: 2.3 g Cholesterol: 5.1 mg

17. EASY HOMEMADE CARAMELS

Prep Time:5 MINUTES

Cook Time:20 MINUTES

Cool down:4 HOURS Total Time:4 HOURS 25 MINUTES

Servings: 80 caramels

Ingredients:

- ½ cup of unsalted butter, plus butter for the pan/parchment paper
- 2 cups of granulated Sugar
- 1 cup of light corn syrup
- 1 tsp kosher salt
- 12 ounces can evaporate milk
- ½ tsp vanilla extract

Instructions:

- To begin, line an 8 x 8-inch pan using parchment paper (for easy removal later.) Make sure the parchment paper is well-coated with butter. The pan should be generously buttered if parchment paper is not available.)
- Liquefy the Butter, Sugar, and corn syrup in a heavy pot over medium heat. The mixture should begin to boil after 5 to 10 minutes of stirring on medium heat.
- Pour the evaporated milk in a slow, steady stream over 12-15 minutes, stirring constantly. Maintaining a steady boil, keep the heat at medium.) Don't rush this process. Patience and time are required.)
- The mixture should be stirred continually, scraping the edges as needed until it achieves a "softball" stage (238 degrees F on a candy thermometer). Pour some hot caramel sauce into an ice water cup and form a ball with your fingers for confirmation. While still a little sticky, it will be firm and malleable when it's done.
- Take from heat when the temperature reaches 238 degrees F / the softball stage. Add a dash of vanilla. As a precaution, it may explode.

Prepared pan:

- Pour mixture into pan. About four hours later, the food is ready to eat. Refrigerate overnight and layout on the counter to warm somewhat at room temperature to keep them refrigerated but not cold. Because of this, cutting them is easier.)

- Lift the parchment paper from the pan to remove the caramels.
- ***Culinary tip***: To make 80 pieces of caramel of identical size, use a sharp knife or a dough/bench scraper to cut the candy into ten rows.
- Twist the ends to seal like a Tootsie roll. Then eat a lot of them or give them away as presents!

Nutrition

Calories: 47kcal | Carbohydrates: 9g | Protein: 1g | Fat: 1g | Saturated Fat: 1g | Cholesterol: 4mg | Sodium: 36mg | Potassium: 13mg | Sugar: 9g | Vitamin A: 46IU | Vitamin C: 1mg | Calcium: 12mg | Iron: 1mg

18. CANDY CANE XMAS POPS

Easy 0:10 Prep 0:02 Cook Makes 14

Ingredients

- 20 candy canes small
- 14 white marshmallows
- 80 g dark chocolate melts

Method

- In a small bowl, combine chocolate melts and microwave on high for 2 minutes or until smooth. Allow cooling for a few minutes.
- Six candy canes crushed in a crusher and pestle. Crush the candy canes and put them in a bowl. You'll want to dip your marshmallows in melted candy canes and gently touch the side of the bowl to remove excess. Crush the

candy canes and roll into them. Line a baking sheet with baking paper and spread out the dough. Recreate this process with all leftover candy canes.

- In order for the candy cane pops to harden, place them in the refrigerator (approximately 15 minutes).

EQUIPMENT

- microwave
- mortar and pestle

NOTES

- This dish can also be made with green or rainbow candy canes.

19. PEPPERMINT BARK OREOS

Ingredients

- One package of Oreo cookies
- One bag of white candy melts
- One bag crushed peppermint candy (or crush your own)
- wax paper
- peppermint bark oreo cookies

Instructions:

- Pour melted chocolate over Oreo cookies and spread on wax paper.

- CRUSH PEPPERMINT CANDY ON TOP OF COOKIE.

- Continue this process with the remaining cookies.

- Let the cookies set completely before serving (about 30 minutes)

20. HOMEMADE PEPPERMINT PATTIES

Prep Time:40 minutes Chilling time1 hour 5 minutes Servings:48 peppermint patties

INGREDIENTS:

- ¼ cup of (60 grams) unsalted butter, softened
- ⅓ cup of (80 ml) light corn syrup
- One and ½ tsp peppermint extract
- Three and ½ cups of (420 grams) powdered sugar plus extra for sprinkling on work surface
- 12 ounces (340 grams) semisweet chocolate roughly chopped

INSTRUCTIONS

- Whip softened butter, light corn syrup, and peppermint extract into a smooth paste with a stand mixer or large mixing basin.
- After the powdered sugar has been incorporated, continue to mix at low speed for a few minutes until the mixture comes together. At first, the mixture will be extremely crumbly. Use your hands to knead the dough as soon as the mixture comes together but is still crumbly.
- A sheet of parchment paper should be sprinkled with powdered sugar before the dough is rolled out onto it. Once you've produced a good ball of dough, it's time to flatten it out with your fingers. Roll out the dough to about ¼ -inch thickness on another piece of parchment paper using a rolling pin.

- Make a large baking sheet by lining it with parchment paper and setting it aside. Cut out dough with a 1.25-1.5 inch round cutter and place on a baking sheet lightly greased with nonstick spray (If the dough is too soft to handle, freeze it for 5-10 minutes). Until all the dough is gone, re-roll and cut scraps into circles.

- Freeze the baking sheets with the cut-out peppermint patties for around 15-20 minutes.
- Chop up the chocolate into a microwavable bowl when the burgers are almost done. In 20-30 second intervals, microwave the mixture, stirring well after each interval until it is completely melted.
- Remove the baking sheet out of the freezer and place it on a baking sheet. Dip each patty into the chocolate, tap off any excess, and carefully place it back on the baking pan (I use a toothpick to slide it off the fork). Make sure to coat all of the remaining patties. Place the patties back in the freezer for 10-15 minutes if they become too soft to dip.
- Place a baking sheet in the refrigerator for about 30 to 45 minutes to harden up the chocolate on all peppermint patties.
- To eat or keep in an airtight container in the refrigerator, simply follow these instructions:

NOTES

- Refrigerate a container of peppermint patties for up to one week.

- Peppermint patties keep nicely in the freezer for up to three months. Refrigerate overnight to thaw.

- If you like, you can substitute dark chocolate or milk chocolate for semisweet chocolate.

21. PEANUT BUTTER TRUFFLES

PREP TIME:10 mins CHILL:30 mins TOTAL TIME: 40 mins SERVINGS:20

EQUIPMENT

- Cookie Scoop

INGREDIENTS

- 1 cup of powdered Sugar
- ½ cup of creamy or chunky peanut butter
- 3 Tbsp butter room temperature
- 16 ounces white melting chocolate
- Sprinkles, melted milk chocolate, or chopped nuts Optional

INSTRUCTIONS

- Add powdered sugar, peanut butter, and butter to a medium bowl and mix until smooth. Stir the items together using a wide spatula.
- Using a tiny portion scoop, cookie scoop, or shaping with hands, make dough balls out of the scoops.
- Refrigerate for 15-30 minutes after placing on parchment paper.
- The chocolate can be heated in the microwave for 30 seconds once the dough has chilled.
- The dough bites should be dipped in melted chocolate and then placed on wax or parchment paper. Allow them to remain until the chocolate has hardened before sprinkling with chosen garnish.

Tips/Notes:

- According to how big you roll them, this recipe yields around 18-20 bites.

- When it comes to the bites, don't worry about them not being perfectly shaped balls. As soon as they've been cold and reshaped, you're ready to dip them in chocolate. For a thicker crust, you can dip them twice.
- Melt the first half of the chocolate. You may not need a complete pound of truffles, depending on the size of your truffles.
- For any new chocolate, On parchment paper, I pour it, then store it in a Ziplock bag.
- Sprinkles, melted white chocolate, shredded coconut, and crushed peanuts were all used to decorate the tops. Before the chocolate has hardened, sprinkle the topping on the freshly dipped truffle.
- In addition, I've utilized colored candy melts for themed events and holidays!

NUTRITION:

Calories: 126kcal | Carbohydrates: 13g | Protein: 2g | Fat: 8g | Saturated Fat: 4g | Cholesterol: 5mg | Sodium: 55mg | Potassium: 42mg | FPound er: 1g | Sugar: 13g | Vitamin A: 52IU | Calcium: 3mg | Iron: 1mg

22. CARAMEL APPLE CHEESECAKE DIP

INGREDIENTS:

serves a crowd

- 8Ounces 1/3 less fat cream cheese, softened to room temperature
- 9Ounces SoDelicious CoCoWhip Topping
- sliced apples
- graham crackers
- For the Caramel Sauce (makes ~1 cup of):

- 1 cup of packed Brown Sugar
- 1/2 cup of half and half
- 1/4 cup of butter
- dash of salt
- 1 Tbsp vanilla

DIRECTIONS:

- A small pot over medium heat should be filled with brown sugar, half-and-half, butter, and sea salt. The mixture should thicken within 8-10 minutes of being brought to a simmer and then reduced to a simmer for another 8-10 minutes. Simmer for two more minutes, frequently stirring, before adding the vanilla. Remove from heat and allow to cool completely; this step can be completed in advance.
- Add 1 cup of caramel sauce to a large bowl of cream cheese and whisk until smooth.
- Reserve 2 Tbsp caramel sauce for the dip's garnish. A spatula is needed to incorporate the whipped topping. The dip should be refrigerated for at least two hours before serving.
- Serve with apple slices and graham crackers by scooping the dip into a serving bowl and topping it with the remaining caramel sauce and broken graham crackers (optional).

NOTES:

Caramel DIP should never be substituted for SAUCE when making homemade caramel.

23. CROCKPOT CANDY CRACK RECIPE

Prep Time: 5 minutesCook Time: 2 hours Total Time: 2 hours 5 minutes

Ingredients:

- 1 16 Ounces jar of salted peanuts
- 1 16 Ounces jar of unsalted peanuts
- 1 12 Ounces bag semisweet chocolate chips
- 1 12 Ounces bag milk chocolate chips
- 2 10 Ounces bag peanut butter chips
- 2 1 lb vanilla candy coating

Instructions

- In a 6-quart slow cooker, place the peanuts first and then layer the rest of the ingredients on top.

- Set the heat to low and place the lid on the pot for two hours.

- It's time to get down to business.

- The mixture should be spooned onto wax paper and allowed to solidify for an hour.

- When stored in an airtight container, it can be kept for up to two weeks at room temperature.

24. CHRISTMAS CANDY COOKIE BARK

PREP TIME: 15 minutes

TOTAL TIME: 15 minutes

SERVINGS: 18 PIECES

Ingredients:

- 16 Ounces. Almond Bark, I use vanilla
- 14 Winter Oreos, chopped into small pieces

- One and 1/2 cups of pretzels, broken into small pieces
- 2/3 cup of red and green M&Ms
- red and green sprinkles

Instructions:

- A 9x13-inch pan should be lined with wax or parchment paper.
- Pretzels, Oreos, and half of the M & Ms should be evenly distributed on the parchment paper.
- Start heating the almond bark for 1 minute and 30 seconds on high in a microwave-safe bowl (I used a glass measuring cup.). Mix and heat for an additional 30 seconds to ensure smoothness. If the mixture is not smooth when stirred, repeat the process and heat for 15 seconds. Avoid overheating.
- Pour the melted almond bark over the pan's contents. Spread the melted bark evenly on top using a rubber spatula.
- The leftover M&Ms and sprinkles can be sprinkled on top of the bark while it is still wet. About two hours later, remove the bark from the pan and place it in the refrigerator.
- Keep the bark in an airtight container by chopping it up with your hands. When not in use, bark can be kept at room temperature or even frozen.

Notes:

- When lining your pan, use parchment paper instead of aluminum foil. It makes clean-up a breeze and protects your bark from adhering to the pan, too.
- The bark should be refrigerated until it is completely firm, at least two hours, before cutting it into pieces.

- Cookie bark can be stored in an airtight container at room temperature for about two to three days. If you like, you can keep it in the refrigerator, but it's acceptable to keep it at room temperature.

Nutritions:

Calories: 252kcal |Sodium: 140mg Carbohydrates: 35g | Protein: 2g | Fat: 11g | Saturated Fat: 9g | Cholesterol: 1mg | | Potassium: 29mg | FPound er: 1g | Sugar: 27g |

25. CHRISTMAS CRACK RECIPE

Prep Time: 5 minsCook Time: 8 minsTotal Time: 13 mins
Servings: 30

Ingredients

- 50 saltine crackers (approx.)
- 1 cup of salted butter (2 sticks, cubed)
- 1 cup of light brown sugar (packed)
- 2 cups of chocolate chips
- 1/2 – 1 cup of M&M's (or chopped nuts or sliced almonds)

Instructions:

- Preheat the oven to 325 degrees Fahrenheit. Aluminum foil a jelly roll pan. Line the pan with saltine crackers after spraying the foil with nonstick-stick cooking spray.
- To begin, melt the butter and sugar together in a medium-sized saucepan over low heat. Stir in the melted butter. After the butter has melted, bring it to a boil for 3 minutes. Continually stir the mixture. Take the pan from the heat once it's bubbling and has turned a darker caramel color. Pour equally over saltine crackers. Spread

the mixture with a knife, but don't worry about getting it exactly right.

- Bake the pan for 7-9 minutes in the oven. As the crackers bake, the mixture will spread evenly across them.
- Pour the melted or melted chocolate over the top with a spatula after removing the pan from the heat source. After 15 minutes, top with M&Ms (or nuts).
- The chocolate will keep for 1–2 weeks if stored in an airtight container after hardened.

Notes:

Variations:

- Make the base using ritz or graham crackers
- Add white chocolate or drizzle white chocolate on top
- Sprinkle with chopped nuts
- Sprinkles can be added for color.

26. CARAMEL MARSHMALLOW POPCORN

PREP TIME 5 minutes

COOK TIME: FIVE minutes

SERVINGS 12 cups

Ingredients:

- 12 cups of popcorn
- ½ cup of butter
- ½ cup of Brown Sugar
- 12 marshmallows (the big ones. NOT miniature)

Instructions:

- In a large bowl, combine popcorn and butter. Ensure that no kernels are left unpopped. Dispose of.
- Liquefy the butter and brown sugar in a saucepan.
- Take off the heat and stir in the salt and vanilla. Stir until the chocolate is melted. Using a spoon, mix in the marshmallows until they are completely dissolved and smooth.
- With a rubber spatula, spread the caramel over the popcorn until it's uniformly coated.

NUTRITION INFORMATION

Calories: 167, Carbohydrates: 23g, Protein: 1g, Fat: 8g, Saturated Fat: 4g, Cholesterol: 20mg, Sodium: 76mg, Potassium: 48mg, FPound er: 1g, Sugar: 13g, Vitamin A: 260IU, Calcium: 10mg, Iron: 0.4mg

27. CHOCOLATE BUTTERSCOTCH HAYSTACKS

Prep: 25 min. + chilling Makes:3 dOuncesen

Ingredients

- 2 cups of semisweet chocolate chips
- One package (10 to 11 ounces) butterscotch chips
- 4 cups of crispy chow mein noodles

Directions

- Melt the chocolate and butterscotch chips, stirring until smooth, in a microwave set over a pot of boiling water. Add the noodles and toss gently.
- To bake, use waxed paper-lined baking sheets and drop by rounded tablespoonfuls. To set, place in the refrigerator for 10-15 minutes.

Nutrition Facts

One cookie: 160 calories, 9g fat (5g saturated fat), 0 cholesterol, 84mg sodium, 22g carbohydrate (15g sugars, 1g f Pounder), 1g protein.

28. OREO BALLS - OREO TRUFFLES

Servings: 36 truffles Prep:25 minutes Cook:5 minutes

Ingredients

- 36 Oreos (original, not double stuff), plus three more, crushed, for topping if desired
- 1 (8 Ounces) package cream cheese, softened
- 16 Ounces vanilla or chocolate candy melts, or melted white chocolate, milk chocolate, or dark chocolate
- See notes for peppermint variation

Instructions

- Using wax paper or parchment paper, cover an 18-by-13-inch baking sheet.
- Place 36 Oreos in a food processor and process until fine crumbs form (don't remove cream filling).
- Add cream cheese and pulse until combined.
- Form the dough into 1-inch balls by scooping out about 1 Tbsp at a time and putting them on the prepared baking sheet.
- Freeze the truffles for 15 minutes before serving. Meanwhile, smash the remaining three Oreos.

- When you're done melting the almond bark or chocolate, put it in an airtight container.
- Using a spoon, pour some melted chocolate over the top of the truffles, then raise the truffles and let the excess chocolate drip off.

- Immediately sprinkle with crumbled Oreos if desired, then let the chocolate harden on the baking sheet.
- Maintain its freshness in the refrigerator by storing it in an airtight container.

Notes:
- If you do not have a food processor, a rolling pin will work.
- A spoon and a mixing bowl are all that is needed if you do not own a mixer.

For The Peppermint Version

- If you use a stand mixer, combine the cream cheese with 1 1/2 tsp of peppermint extract first, then proceed as suggested.

- DIP THE CHOCOLATES AND IMMEDIATELY SPRINKLE THE TOPS WITH CRUSHED CANDY CANES OR STARLIGHT MINTS, OR CRUSHED PEPPERMINT BITS (INSTEAD OF MORE CRUSHED OREOS).

29. RASPBERRY NO-BAKE CHEESECAKE

PREP TIME:15 mins

TOTAL TIME:15 mins SERVINGS:8

INGREDIENTS:

Chocolate Cookie Crust
- 1 cup of chocolate sandwich cookies filling removed and crushed
- 3 tbsp unsalted butter melted

Cream Cheese Filling

- 8 ounces cream cheese softened
- 1 ½ cups of fresh raspberries, divided (about ½ pint) plus extra for decorating
- ¾ cup of powdered sugar sifted
- 2 cups of heavy whipping cream (or 16 Ounces tub of whipped topping)

INSTRUCTIONS:

Cookie Crust

- In a medium-sized mixing dish, combine cookie crumbs and melted butter. The bottom of a 9-inch springform pan should be firmly pressed down. Refrigerate until ready to use.

Cream Cheese Filling

- Whisk softened cream cheese and powdered sugar in a large mixing bowl with 1 cup of fresh raspberries. Whip heavy cream until stiff. Fold in the raspberry cream cheese mixture with care. Spoon over the chilled chocolate crust and use a spatula to smooth out any air bubbles.
- Preserve for an hour before serving. Freeze for four hours before serving. If preferred, garnish the dish with more fresh raspberries right before serving. Within 24 hours, the best is done.

NOTES

- Graham cracker crumbs can be substituted for chocolate sandwich cookies.

- A 16-ounce tub of Cool Whip can be substituted for the heavy whipping cream if you don't want to create your own.

- Chill time is not counted in the total time (about 4 hours).

- Blending is easier if the cream cheese is at room temperature.

- Sift the powdered sugar.

- Fresh raspberries can be added just before serving (and mint leaves, if desired)

- Refrigerate the raspberry no-bake cheesecake after it has been made, wrapped with plastic wrap. After 24 hours, the mixture may dry up and fracture a little bit.

30. OREO PEPPERMINT BARK

Prep Time:15 minutes

Total Time:15 minutes Servings: 20 pieces

Ingredients

- 10 ounces white chocolate melting wafers
- ½ tsp peppermint extract
- Ten oreo cookies crushed
- 2 tbsp sprinkles

Instructions

- Add the wafers to a microwave-safe bowl and microwave on high for 1 minute. In 30 second intervals, microwave, stirring every time, until a smooth, melted consistency is achieved.
- Stir in the peppermint extract until it's completely dissolved. Coat the cookie dough with crushed Oreos and mix thoroughly (mixture will be thick).

- A 10-12 inch oval, about ¼ inch thick, should be spread onto a parchment-lined baking sheet. Decorate while the candy is still wet with sprinkles.
- Remove from oven and cool for 15 minutes in the refrigerator. Bring to room temperature and cut into 2-inch squares.

Equipment Recommendations:

- Parchment Paper
- Half Baking Sheet
- Pyrex Glass Mixing Bowls
- Measuring Spoons

Notes

- At room temperature, candy bark can be stored in a tightly sealed container for up to two weeks, and in the freezer, IT CAN BE STORED FOR UP TO SIX MONTHS.

31. PEPPERMINT BARK PUPPY CHOW

Ingredients:

6-7 Cups of Rice Chex cereal

2 Cups of White Melts Or Almond Bark*

1 and 3/4 C. crushed candy canes about 15 or so

Use something that can be melted and used for candy, as white chocolate chips don't melt down thin enough.

Instructions

- In a big bowl, mix the cereal and the melted white melts or almond bark.
- Stir until the mixture is smooth.

- Fold in the melted goodness until the cereal is well covered.
- A large plastic bag (or Tupperware container with a lid) and crushed candy canes are all that's needed. Hand-mix until all components are mixed.
- Bake on a baking sheet until they're ready to eat!

NOTE:

- You may always adjust the sweetness by adding more or less chocolate or cereal.
- • Puppy chow/muddy pals aren't an exact science.

IDEA:

- To share with family and friends, place the food in lovely Christmas goody bags.

32. PEPPERMINT RICE KRISPIES TREATS

Prep Time:15 mins

Cook Time:3 mins

Total Time:18 mins Servings: 9 people

Ingredients:

- 4 Tbsp unsalted butter
- 12 Ounces package mini marshmallows
- 2 drops peppermint extract
- 6 cups of Rice Krispies cereal
- 1 cup of white chocolate chips
- Six peppermint candies crushed

Instructions

- ALUMINUM FOIL OR PARCHMENT PAPER A 13-BY-9-INCH BAKING DISH DISPOSE OF.

- GREASE A BIG BOWL WITH BUTTER AND SET IT ASIDE. A BOWL OF CEREAL SHOULD BE READY.

- •The butter should be melted in a medium-sized saucepan.

- Stir in marshmallows and cook until they are nearly melted.

- TO ENSURE THAT ALL MARSHMALLOWS ARE MELTED, REMOVE FROM HEAT, ADD EXTRACT, AND STIR THOROUGHLY.

- Toss the cereal with the mixture and eat it. Toss to coat.

Prepared pan:

- Press cereal mixture into pan. Gently press down on the top.

- PREFERABLY ROOM TEMPERATURE BEFORE SERVING.

- MICROWAVE THE CHOCOLATE IN A SAFE BASIN.

- Mix until smooth.

- Rice Krispie treats are coated with the frosting.

- Sprinkle the chocolate with crushed peppermint candy.

- Allow the chocolate to harden before serving.

- Serve by cutting into bars.

- A SEALED CONTAINER CAN BE REFRIGERATED FOR A WEEK.

33. ROLO PRETZEL TURTLES

READY IN:10 mins SERVES:8 YIELD: 30 cookies

INGREDIENTS

- 30 Rolo chocolates
- 30 small pretzels (not sticks, but the flat, figure-8 shaped kind)
- 30 pecans or 30 walnuts, toasted

DIRECTIONS

- THE OVEN SHOULD BE Warm up to 350 DEGREES FAHRENHEIT.

- Discard the ROLES. Bake the pretzels with ROLES ON TOP OF A BAKING SHEET.

- TAKE OUT OF THE Micro oven AND ALLOW IT TO COOL FOR ABOUT 5 MINUTES. AS LONG AS IT HASN'T BEEN FULLY DEMOLISHED, THE Rolo is still edible.

- Squish the chocolate with a nut as soon as it comes out of the oven. Keep an eye out for the caramel OUNCES. YUM.

CHAPTER 4:CAKE, PIES, DESSERTS:

34. EASY BREAD PUDDING

Cook Time: 50 minutes

Total Time: One hour 50 minutes Yield: 9

Ingredients:
For the Bread Pudding

- 6 cups of cubed stale bread (french, challah, brioche, regular sliced)
- 2 cups of milk
- Three large eggs
- 1 cup of (207g) sugar
- 2 tbsp butter, melted
- 1 1/2 tbsp vanilla extract
- 1 tsp ground cinnamon
- 1/2 tsp nutmeg
- For the Vanilla Sauce
- 1/2 cup of butter
- 1 cup of Sugar
- 1/2 cup of heavy whipping cream
- 1 tbsp vanilla extract

Instructions

- Get an 8x8-inch casserole dish and lay it aside for later.
- It's best if the bottom of the casserole dish is covered with a thin layer of breadcrumbs.
- Gather all of the ingredients for the pudding in a large bowl and whisk them together. Assemble the bread in the mixture.
- Set aside 20-25 minutes to soak the bread.
- The oven should be Warm up to 350°F (176°C) in the meantime. It should take between 50 and 55 minutes to bake. While it should have some wiggle, it should be stable. For the middle to rise entirely, it may need a little longer time in the oven. Remove from the oven when done.
- Make the vanilla sauce while the bread pudding is cooking. Using a medium pot, melt the butter, add the sugar, cream, and vanilla essence and stir until the sugar is completely dissolved.

- Finish cooking when the mixture coats a spoon.
- Carefully remove it from the heat, spoon it over the bread pudding.

Notes

For a 9x13 pan, use one-and-a-half recipes worth of the ingredients

35. CLASSIC APPLE CRISP

Prep Time: 15 minutes

Cook Time: 45 minutes

Yield: serves 8-10

Ingredients
Filling

- Eight medium apples, cut into 1-inch chunks that are 1/4 – 1/2 inch thick (about 10 cups of chunks)
- 1/2 cup of (100g) packed light or dark brown Sugar
- 1/4 cup of (31g) all-purpose flour (spoon & leveled)
- 1 tsp pure vanilla extract
- 1 tsp ground cinnamon
- 1/2 tsp ground nutmeg
- 1/4 tsp salt

Topping

- 3/4 cup of (94g) all-purpose flour (spoon & leveled)
- 3/4 cup of (150g) packed light or dark brown Sugar
- 1 tsp ground cinnamon
- 1/2 cup of (1 stick; 115g) unsalted butter, cold and cubed
- 1 cup of old-fashioned whole oats

Instructions:

- Warm up the oven to 350°F (177°C). A 9x13-inch baking pan should be lightly greased. Any four-quart baking dish will do.
- Mix all filling ingredients in a large dish and distribute evenly in the baking pan.

Make the topping:

- In a bigger bowl, combine the flour, brown sugar, and cinnamon. Crumble the butter into the mixture with a pastry cutter or a fork. Add the oats and mix.
- Overlay the filling and bake for 45 minutes, or until golden brown and bubbling around the edges. At least five minutes after removing it from the oven, lay the dish on a wire rack to cool completely. Plain or salted caramel and vanilla ice cream can be served warm, room temperature, or cold.
- Refrigerate leftovers firmly wrapped for up to five days.

Notes

- PREPARE AHEAD OF TIME & FREEZE THE CRISP CAN BE FROZEN FOR UP TO THREE MONTHS ONCE IT HAS BEEN BAKED AND COOLED. COOK AT 350°F (177°C) FOR 30 MINUTES OR UNTIL COOKED THROUGH AFTER THAWING OVERNIGHT IN THE REFRIGERATOR. AFTERWARDS, YOU CAN COVER AND REFRIGERATE IT FOR UP TO A DAY TO ENSURE THE CRISP IS READY TO BAKE. THE UNBAKED CRISP WILL KEEP IN THE FREEZER FOR UP TO THREE MONTHS. STEP 4: THAW IN THE REFRIGERATOR OVERNIGHT, THEN PROCEED WITH STEP 3. BECAUSE THE CRISP IS CHILLED, IT WILL TAKE LONGER TO BAKE.

- My favorite apples for apple crisp are Granny Smith and Jazz or Pink Lady.

- FOR OATMEAL, YOU CAN USE QUICK OR WHOLE OATS, DEPENDING ON YOUR PREFERENCE. ONLY A LITTLE MORE POWDERED, THE CRUMBLE TOPPING. AVOID REDUCING THE FLOUR SINCE IT COULD MAKE YOUR TOPPING OILY. A SIMPLE TRANSITION FROM WHOLE OATS TO SHORT-GRAIN OATS IS ALL THAT IS NEEDED. SEE THE BLOG POST ABOVE FOR A RECIPE FOR A NUT-FREE OAT TOPPING.

- Pecan or walnuts can be added to the crisp topping if desired. When you add the oats, stir them in.

- Half Recipe: To make this recipe in a 9-inch square or round baking dish, simply divide the ingredients in half. Bake for roughly 30 to 35 minutes less.

36. CHERRY-ALMOND-CREAM CHEESE CRESCENT DANISH TREE

Prep:15 Min Total:35 Min Ingredients:7 Servings:11

Ingredients
Danish and Filling

- One can (8 Ounces) refrigerated Pillsbury™ Original Crescent Rolls (8 Count) or one can (8 Ounces) refrigerated Pillsbury™ Original Crescent Dough Sheet
- 2 Ounces (from 8-Ounces package) cream cheese, softened
- 1/4 cup of powdered Sugar
- 1/8 tsp almond extract
- 1/4 cup of canned cherry pie filling (from 21-Ounces can)

Topping

- 1/4 cup of powdered Sugar
- 1 to 1 1/2 tsp milk

Steps:

- Take the oven temperature to 375 degrees. The cooking parchment paper should be used to cover a big cookie sheet. Don't deflate or unroll the dough. Cut the dough roll in half with a serrated knife, then each half into 11 sections.
- The dough should be laid out in the shape of a tree on a cookie sheet, with a round at the bottom to serve as the tree's foundation. The middle of each round should be gently pressed to form a well for toppings.
- The cream cheese, powdered sugar, and almond essence should be combined with a spoon in a small bowl. Spread a little amount of the cream cheese mixture onto the center of each round of dough. One cherry on top of each. The dough should be golden brown and baked through after baking for 16 to 19 minutes.
- To make the drizzling sauce, combine 1/4 cup of powdered sugar and 1 tsp of milk in an airtight container and shake to combine. Spritz the crescent tree with the topping and serve it warm.

Tips:

- Cherry pie filling can be used to top desserts like brownies or ice cream.

- Danishes are best served the day they are made.

37. PERFECT PUMPKIN PIE

Servings: 8 to 10 (Makes one 9-inch deep-dish pie)

Prep Time: 30 Minutes

Cook Time: One Hour 45 Minutes

Total Time: Two Hours 15 Minutes, plus time to chill the dough and cool the pie

INGREDIENTS:

- 1 (9-inch) Homemade Pie Crust or deep-dish frOuncesen pie crust shell (thawed)
- 1 (15-Ounces) can pure pumpkin (about 1-3/4 cups of)
- One large egg
- Three large eggs yolks
- 1/2 cup of granulated Sugar
- 1/2 cup of light brown sugar, wrapped in a plastic bag
- 2 tbsp all-purpose flour
- 1/2 tsp salt
- 1 tsp ground cinnamon
- 1 tsp ground ginger
- 1/2 tsp ground nutmeg
- 1/8 tsp ground cloves
- 1/8 tsp ground black pepper
- 1-1/4 cups of evaporated milk (you'll need one 12-Ounces can, but you won't use all of it)

INSTRUCTIONS

- Assemble the ingredients and preheat the oven to 375°F.

- If you're making your pie crust, wrap it in parchment paper and refrigerate it until firm. Dried beans or pie weights can be used to fill the crust up to three-quarters of the way. Twenty minutes in the oven should do it. To remove the parchment paper and beans/pie weights, take the crust from the oven; fold a couple of lengthwise-folded strips of foil over the edges (this will protect the edges from getting too dark). The dough should be dry and golden after another 20 minutes of baking. Using a flat spatula, like a pancake turner, gently press down on the puffed-up bottom, taking care not to pierce it. Don't throw away the foil just yet; you may use it again.
- If you're using a frozen crust, make sure to blind bake it according to the package directions.
- Reduce the oven's temperature to 325°F after the crust has been blind-baked.

Make the Pumpkin Pie Filling:

- A large bowl should be used to mash the pumpkin with the eggs, yolks, and Sugar (both granulated and brown), flour, salt, and spices are all included in this recipe. Serve with vanilla ice cream or a scoop of ice cream.
- It should take between 50 and 60 minutes for the filling to set. The borders should be dry, but the middle should wobble slightly if you shake the pan. Inspect the pie as it bakes, and if the crust appears to be browning too quickly, use the foil strips to cover the edges again. For a few hours, let the pie cool completely at room temperature on a wire rack (instead of in the oven). Refrigerate until ready to serve, or slice and serve.

Make-Ahead:

- It is possible to make the pumpkin pie up to one day in advance and store it in the refrigerator.

Freezer-Friendly Instructions:

- TO KEEP THE DOUGH FRESH FOR UP TO TWO DAYS OR FOR UP TO A MONTH, PACK IT IN PLASTIC AND REFRIGERATE. IF YOU'VE FROZEN IT, LET IT THAW IN THE FRIDGE OVERNIGHT. WHEN THE PIE HAS BEEN BAKED FOR UP TO A MONTH, IT CAN BE FROZEN. WRAP IT IN ALUMINUM FOIL OR PLASTIC FREEZER WRAP, OR PUT IT IN A HEAVY-DUTY FREEZER BAG AFTER IT HAS COOLED FULLY. FIRST, THAW IT IN THE REFRIGERATOR OVERNIGHT BEFORE SERVING IT.

38. PUMPKIN BARS

Prep: 20 min. Bake: 25 min. + cooling Makes two dOuncesen

Ingredients

- Four large eggs, room temperature
- 1-2/3 cups of Sugar
- 1 cup of canola oil
- One can (15 ounces) pumpkin
- 2 cups of all-purpose flour
- 2 tsp ground cinnamon
- 2 tsp baking powder
- 1 tsp baking soda
- 1 tsp salt

icing:

- 6 ounces cream cheese, softened
- 2 cups of confectioners' Sugar

- 1/4 cup of Kerrygold Salted Butter, softened
- 1 tsp vanilla extract
- 1 to 2 tbsp 2% milk

Directions

- Make an egg white omelet by whisking the egg whites with sugar, oil, and pumpkin. When you're ready to bake, combine the flour and baking powder and gradually add it to the pumpkin mixture while mixing thoroughly. Pour into a 15x10x1-inch baking pan that has been left uncoated. At 350 degrees Fahrenheit, bake for 25 to 30 minutes, or until the pudding is set. Completely cool down.
- A tiny bowl is all that's needed for the icing, which consists of cream cheese, confectioners' Sugar, butter, and vanilla. To get spreading consistency, add enough milk. Decorate the bars with frosting. Keep in the fridge.

Nutrition Facts

One bar: 260 calories, 13g fat (3g saturated fat), 45mg cholesterol, 226mg sodium, 34g carbohydrate (24g sugars, 1g f Pounder), 3g protein.

39. CHOCOLATE CHIP COOKIE PIE CRUST

Total: 10 min Active: 10 min Yield: 1 pie crust

Ingredients:

- 12 crispy chocolate chip cookies, store-bought or homemade and overbaked (see Cook's Note)
- 1 tbsp dark brown Sugar
- 1 tsp ground cinnamon
- 1 tbsp butter, melted

Directions:

- When you're done pulverizing the cookies, transfer them to a bowl. Make sure to whisk in the brown sugar and cinnamon. Pour in the melted butter and whisk until the cookies are well coated.

- TO PRODUCE A PIE CRUST, PRESS THE MIXTURE INTO A 9-INCH PIE PLATE, MAKING SURE THAT ALL THE SURFACES ARE EQUAL. BEFORE ADDING THE FILLING TO A NO-BAKE PIE, BAKE THE CRUST: TEN MINUTES AT 375 DEGREES FAHRENHEIT SHOULD DO THE TRICK; THE EXACT DURATION WILL DEPEND ON HOW CRISPY YOUR COOKIES ARE. IF YOU ARE MAKING A BAKED PIE, DO NOT PRE-COOK THE CRUST. ADD THE FILLING AND FOLLOW THE RECIPE'S INSTRUCTIONS FOR COOKING THE PIE.

40. MONKEY BREAD

YIELDS: 8 servings PREP TIME: 0 hours 20 mins COOK TIME: 0 hours 40 mins TOTAL TIME:1 hour 0 mins

Ingredients:

- Three cans of buttermilk biscuits (the non-flaky ones)
- One c. sugar
- 2 tsp. (to 3 tsp) cinnamon
- Two sticks butter
- 1/2 c. Brown Sugar

Directions:

- SET THE Micro oven TEMPERATURE TO 350 DEGREES FAHRENHEIT.

- All three cans of biscuits should be opened, and each biscuit should be sliced in half.

- WHITE SUGAR AND 2-3 TSP. CINNAMON IS NEXT. IT HAS A STRONG CINNAMON FLAVOR BECAUSE OF THE 3 TSP OF CINNAMON IN IT. IF CINNAMON ISN'T YOUR THING, REDUCE THE AMOUNT TO 2 TSP. SHAKE THE INGREDIENTS IN A 1-GALLON ZIP-TOP BAG TO ENSURE THEY ARE WELL-COMBINED.

- IN A BOWL, COMBINE THE CINNAMON-SUGAR MIXTURE AND THE BISCUIT QUARTERS. SEAL THE BAG AND SHAKE VIGOROUSLY ONCE ALL THE BISCUIT QUARTERS HAVE BEEN ADDED. THEY'LL COME APART AND BE COATED IN CINNAMON SUGAR AS A RESULT OF THIS METHOD. IN THE bundt pan, distribute the nuggets equally.

- THE TWO STICKS OF BUTTER AND ½ CUP OF BROWN SUGAR WILL NEED TO BE MELTED IN A SAUCEPAN OVER MEDIUM-HIGH HEAT AT THIS TIME. USE BROWN SUGAR, LIGHT OR DARK. BUTTER AND SUGAR SHOULD BE COOKED TOGETHER FOR A FEW MINUTES WITH CONSTANT STIRRING UNTIL THEY ARE FULLY INCORPORATED. POUR THE BROWN SUGAR BUTTER OVER THE BISCUITS ONCE IT HAS BECOME UNIFORM IN COLOR.

- THE CRUST SHOULD BE A DEEP, DARK BROWN, AND CRISPY AFTER BAKING FOR 30-40 MINUTES. TAKE IT OUT OF THE OVEN WHEN IT'S DONE BAKING. PREFERABLY 15 TO 30 MINUTES OF COOLING TIME BEFORE TRANSFERRING TO SERVING DISH.

41. FROUNCESEN YORK PEPPERMINT PATTY PIE

SERVES:1- 9" pie PREP TIME:10 Min

Ingredients:

- 1 Oreo chocolate crumb pie crust
- 2/3 c International Delight Peppermint Patty flavored coffee creamer liquid
- 4 ounces cream cheese, room temperature
- 2 c Cool Whip
- One dark chocolate candy bar for shaving in and on pie

How To Make:

- Cream cheese should be whipped until it is light and fluffy.
- Gradually add coffee creamer to your brew.
- Stir in the Cool Whip until the mixture is completely smooth.
- To make a chocolate pie, grate 2 ounces of chocolate and mix in 1 ounce (more if you want).
- The mixture should be placed in a pie crust. Top with the remaining chocolate shavings.
- Freeze until ready to serve.
- Cover and freeze.

Printed in Great Britain
by Amazon

53773445R00036